THE HISTORY AND TECHNIQUES
OF THE GREAT MASTERS

DEGAS

THE HISTORY AND TECHNIQUES OF THE GREAT MASTERS

DEGAS

Linda Bolton

CHARTWELL
BOOKS, INC.

A QUARTO BOOK

Published by Chartwell Books
A Division of Book Sales, Inc.
110 Enterprise Avenue
Secaucus, New Jersey 07094

ISBN 1-55521-262-X

This book was designed and produced by
Quarto Publishing plc
The Old Brewery, 6 Blundell Street
London N7 9BH

Project Editor Hazel Harrison
Designer Terry Smith
Picture Researcher Carina Dvorak

Art Director Moira Clinch
Editorial Director Carolyn King

Typeset by QV Typesetting Ltd
Manufactured in Hong Kong by Regent
Publishing Services Limited
Printed in Hong Kong by Leefung-Asco
Printers Ltd

CONTENTS

INTRODUCTION

EDGAR DEGAS
Self-portrait
1885
Louvre, Paris

"Art is vice," wrote Degas, "one doesn't take it in lawful wedlock, one rapes it." This passionate statement from a man whose art and character are customarily described as detached exposes the paradox of Edgar Degas. It also describes the artist's radical and dramatic approach to picture making, which made him one of the greatest artists of the nineteenth century.

Degas the man

"An original fellow, this Degas, sickly, neurotic, and so myopic that he is afraid of losing his sight; but for this very reason an eminently receptive creature and sensitive to the character of things." Edmond de Goncourt's journal entry expresses something of Degas' contradictory nature: a reactionary with radical ideas, an anti-Semite whose closest friends were Jewish, and a misogynist whose life was spent observing and painting women. He was a man who wished to be simultaneously famous and unknown.

Demanding, difficult and exacting, Degas commanded reverential respect among a small group of close family friends, who put up with his authoritarian stipulations, such as this one, for dinner: "There will be a dish cooked without butter for me. No flowers on the table, very little light...You'll shut up the cat, I know, and no one will bring a dog. And if there are women there, ask them not to put smells on themselves...Scent, when there are things that smell so good! such as toast, for example. And we shall sit down to table at exactly half-past seven."

Degas himself was well aware of the problems of his difficult nature. He remarked to Renoir that he had "one terrible, irreconcilable enemy." "And who," asked Renoir, "is that?" "Why, don't you know? Myself, of course." To another friend he apologized for his harshness while attempting to explain it: "I was, or appeared to be, hard with everyone, owing to a sort of tendency towards roughness that originated in my doubts and my bad temper. I felt I was so inept, so badly equipped, so flabby, while it seemed to me that my calculations regarding art were so accurate, I was sulky with the whole world and with myself."

Degas shielded himself from certain emotional responses. He felt a lack of passion for what is generally held to be the proper sphere for emotion, such as romantic love, baldly stating, "I have no passion." This was, of course, untrue: his emotion was roused by what might be termed the negative passions; he possessed, in inversion, an overendowment of spleen. Should he disagree with a point made in argument his sarcasm was lacerating, and eventually he had to keep silent for fear of exploding.

Those who knew him well saw Degas' brusque exterior as a form of protection. "He carefully hid his sensibility under a mask of iron. He did not easily give his friendship, but when given, his affection was deep, certain, devoted," wrote Pierre Lafond.

"What a creature he was, that Degas!" remarked the picture dealer Paul Gimpel to Renoir, who replied, "All his friends had to leave him; I was one of the last to go, but even I couldn't stay till the end. The incomprehensible thing is that Monet, so gentle and affectionate, was always attacked, whereas Degas, so vitriolic, violent and uncompromising, was accepted from the very first by the Academy, the public and the revolutionaries." "People were afraid of him," was Gimpel's succinct explanation.

Famous for his intellectual rigor, his quick wit and acerbic quips, Degas was a formidable figure respected throughout the artistic world; an artist's artist who was also popular with the picture-buying public. His artistic integrity also made him a frequently emulated artist. "Everyone copies Degas," remarked Gauguin.

In many ways Degas' character and his art are comparable to that of Michelangelo. Both were widely held to be the greatest artists of their day. Both seemed to have suppressed the channels receptive to romantic love ("I

AUGUSTE-DOMINIQUE INGRES
The Gatteaux Family
1850
Louvre, Paris

Degas had a lifelong admiration for Ingres. First introduced to his work through pictures owned by family friends, his respect for the master was fostered at the Atelier Lamothe. By the end of his life he owned some twenty paintings and ninety drawings by Ingres, and he often recounted the story of their one meeting, when Ingres had advised him to "draw lines, young man, a great many lines."

am blocked, impotent," Degas stated). Both appear to have possessed melancholy, prickly characters, prone to spasms of irritation, and both suffered the loss of a mother at an impressionable age, giving rise in this century to posthumous Freudian analysis of the damaging consequences on the psyche occasioned by such dramatic maternal deprivation. Both assumed protective masks, and put all their energy into their art. Furthermore, both men reveal, in their art and in their poetry, a positive leaning toward distress, tension and countertension.

The artist's early life
The events of Degas' life, unlike those of Delacroix or Gauguin, are not of dramatic or romantic interest. He abhorred bohemianism, retaining, to the end of his life, the reserve of his *haute-bourgeoise* upbringing. Born Hilaire Germain Edgar de Gas in Paris on July 19, 1834, Degas, as he later chose to modify his aristocratic surname, was the eldest of five surviving children. His earliest years seem tinged with the melancholy which was to color his life, and which seemed to overshadow the whole Degas household. He appears to have passed a privileged but joyless childhood. His mother, a Creole of French descent, born in New Orleans, educated in France and married at the age of sixteen, also reflects this melancholy as she felt her youth passing "without a single ball." Her married life, given over to childbearing

and domestic duties, ended when Degas was thirteen; she died after the birth of her seventh child.

From the age of eleven Degas boarded at the Lycée Louis-le-Grand, one of only three schools which prepared its pupils for France's élite educational establishment, the Ecole Normale Supérieure. It was here that Degas met other pupils from the same social background, the Halévys, the Rouarts and Paul Valpinçon, with whom he remained lifelong friends.

Education at the lycée was entirely in the classics, with a conspicuous absence of science or math. The poet Paul Valéry described its atmosphere as follows. "Neither cleanliness, nor the smallest notion of hygiene, nor deportment, nor even the pronunciation of our language, had any place in the program of that incredible system, conceived as it was to exclude carefully every-

EDGAR DEGAS
Marguerite Degas in Confirmation Dress
1854
Louvre, Paris

Degas was one of five surviving children, and made many drawings and sketches of his siblings. This early portrait of his sister demonstrates why Degas' father believed that portraiture would become the finest jewel in his son's crown. Like Ingres, Degas used a hard pencil to create light, clear line drawings with little shading.

UTAMARO
The Poem of the Pillow
1788
Victoria and Albert Museum, London

Degas, like many avant-garde artists, found a source of inspiration in the Japanese prints which were beginning to come into the country in large numbers in the mid-nineteenth century. The dramatic cropping of figures, the use of color and pattern and the rejection of tonal modeling and shadow can all be seen in Degas' work.

thing to do with the body, the senses, the sky, the arts, or social life." It did, however, engender a profound respect for the intellect.

On leaving the lycée, Degas complied with his father's instructions to study law, but after only a year he discontinued his studies, determined to become an artist. Such was his devotion to his calling that, following a family row, he is reputed to have abandoned home for a draughty garret. His father was sufficiently impressed with his single-mindedness to agree to him following an artistic training, and seems henceforth to have taken his son's endeavors seriously, as his letters to Degas in Italy testify. In 1855, at the suggestion of Henri Valpinçon, father of his schoolfriend Paul, Degas entered the studio of Louis Lamothe, an obscure artist who had in his youth been a pupil of Ingres.

Artistic training

The year spent in the Atelier Lamothe evidently inculcated in the young Degas a profound respect for Ingres, whom he met through M. Valpincon. This never diminished, and was fostered in the following months by a stint at the principal academic art institution in Paris, the Ecole des Beaux Arts. Although he did not enjoy the Ecole, he was happy with the instruction, which placed great weight on drawing and the copying of engravings and plaster casts of antique works. In the Louvre Degas studied not only the works of the Old Masters, but also those of the more modern painters, absorbing the lessons of Ingres and, to a lesser extent, Delacroix's use of color and Courbet's realism. In 1856, abandoning the Ecole, Degas set off for Italy to complete his artistic tuition independently.

The three years spent in Italy were, wrote Degas "the most extraordinary period of my life." It was the birthplace of his father and home of many Italian relatives. Degas spent his time principally in Naples and Florence, where he had relatives, and Rome, where the French artistic colony grouped around the French Academy in the Villa Medici. Italy was the artistic goal for all aspiring artists, and Degas, of independent means and now free from the pressures of the art institutions, studied the paintings in the galleries, drew his relatives and discussed art and life with fellow countrymen. By his return to France in 1859 he had passed a self-regulated period of observation and study, and had seen at firsthand the European masterpieces in the principal Italian collections.

Degas' earliest finished paintings are highly accomplished family portraits showing considerable psychological insights. Established in Paris, he now dutifully embarked on the large-scale history paintings which were considered, in the mid-nineteenth century, to be the most elevated art form — until the challenge of the avant-garde brought about a reconsideration of the role of this kind of painting. His early works in the genre, *The Misfortunes of the City of Orléans*, *Jephthah's Daughter*, *Spartan Boys and Girls Exercising* and *Semiramis Constructing a City*, all painted between 1860 and 1864, can be loosely termed academic, in the established tradition of nineteenth-century French Salon painting, though *Spartan Boys and Girls*, painted in 1860, shows something of the Degas to come. In this work he has attempted to reinterpret a classical subject in a more modern way, displaying a deliberate ungainliness, a lighter palette and visible brushwork.

The realist painter
By about the mid-1860s Degas had rejected history painting, and had become what he was to remain — a painter of contemporary life. Inspired by the new currents in French painting and by his friendship with Manet — whom he met in the Louvre in 1862 — and the circle of artists at the Café Guerbois, later to become known as the Impressionists, Degas completely changed his subject-matter. He executed fewer portraits, and began to frequent the popular haunts of the man-about-town, making the racecourse and the ballet very much his own.

Although Degas is seldom regarded as an Impressionist painter, he did exhibit with the group, and was

EDGAR DEGAS
Vicomte Lepic and his Daughters, Place de la Concorde
c 1876

This painting, which was lost — presumably destroyed in World War Two — reflects the influence of Japanese prints in the way the figures are cropped at the edge of the canvas. It is both a picture of contemporary life and a lively portrait of a friend, out walking with his daughters and his dog, and captured with the artificially contrived naturalism that became the hallmark of Degas' work.

instrumental in organizing the Impressionist Exhibitions in the 1870s and '80s, which posed a challenge to the accepted artistic standards of the Salon. He shared with the Impressionists an interest in depicting contemporary subject matter, in painting techniques, in Japanese prints, and in light. Where he differed from them was in his preference for artificial lighting and his active dislike of outdoor *(plein-air)* painting, which caused him to remark "The gendarmes should shoot down all those easels cluttering up the countryside."

As an intellectual painter and an artist preoccupied with formal qualities of abstraction, he was not interested in the Impressionists' attempts to record the immediate and transient effects of light, and he had a strong preference for painting people. A classically educated, native Parisian, he had no interest in landscape painting; the calm of the countryside bored him profoundly. Apart from two series of landscapes, the first made around 1869 in Boulogne and a second late in his life, in his studio, his racing scenes are the only works which include a rural background. He also found the painting

of still lifes incomprehensible. It is part of the Degas paradox that, while he needed to work alone, it was people and movement only which interested him. To a greater extent than the Impressionists he strove to reinvent the Old Masters. "Oh Giotto," he implored, "show me how to see Paris, and Paris show me how to see Giotto."

Always dissatisfied with his pictures, he would frequently borrow back sold canvases and rework them — owners of Degas' paintings were rumored to chain them to the wall. Within his chosen range of subjects he repeatedly painted the same thing, making pairs or threes on a single theme, and drawing the subject countless times. One entire notebook was used for a study of the hands for a portrait. He often repeated the remark Ingres had made to him: "Draw lines, young man, a great many lines." Degas himself voiced similar sentiments: "One must treat the same subject ten times, a hundred times." It was part of his working method. He had not time, he maintained, for inspiration. "What I do is the result of reflection and study of the great masters; of inspiration, spontaneity, temperament I know nothing."

EDGAR DEGAS
After the Bath
1880
National Gallery, London

Women washing or bathing was one of Degas' favorite themes, and he painted every aspect of their most intimate ablutions. This is a late work, done in pastel, a medium Degas favored more and more as his eyesight deteriorated. The use of cream-colored paper has given a pervading sense of warmth and unified the colors, while the varied marks of the pastels evoke the different textures.

EDGAR DEGAS
At the Milliners
c 1882
Nelson-Atkins Museum of Art,
Kansas City

Degas was fascinated both by
the young milliners
themselves and by the
customers trying on hats in
front of the mirror. When

asked by a woman who had
accompanied him to the
hat-shop what he found so
interesting he replied, "the
little milliners' red hands." As
in many of Degas' paintings,
we feel that we are spying on
an intimate scene, with the
subjects quite unaware that
they are being watched.

Drawing was the prime concern. It was drawing which led to an understanding of the subject so that the artist could synthesize and stylize. The model should be scrutinized and then painted from memory. "Place the model on the ground floor and paint her from the first floor," he once advised an aspiring artist. He regarded as regrettable that too many artists followed color instead of line, and told the English artist Walter Sickert, "I always tried to urge my colleagues along the path of draftsmanship, which I consider a more fruitful field than that of color." It was through line only, Degas felt, that an understanding of underlying forces could be achieved. Yet toward the end of his life the great draftsman had liberated himself from "the tyranny of line" to become a truly great colorist.

Experiments with media

In the 1870s Degas began to experiment with pastel, a medium which had at the time fallen into disfavor. It offered him the possibility of simultaneous line and color: "I am a colorist with line," he maintained. This aphorism also played upon the apparent contradiction of uniting the two, highlighting the battle between divergent artistic camps — the classical Ingrists and their stress on line, and the Delacroix school of Romantics, who upheld the expressive, emotional effect of color. Degas' liberation derived, in part, from his relentless experimentation, during his forties, with the picture-making process, and with the media of painting and printing techniques.

Degas disliked the shine and consistency of thick oil pigment. He applied his paint thinly, often removing the oil from it, and applying it with turpentine in thin washes of color. He softened his pastels over steam, often making them into paste, and used them in novel combinations over gouache and monotype. He frequently painted with oils on paper, rather than canvas, which not only gave his preferred matte surface as the paper

EDGAR DEGAS
Mary Cassatt at the Louvre
1879-80
Chicago Art Institute

This print shows Degas' radical approach to picture making — both in its dramatic composition and in the range of printing techniques used. From the mid-1870s Degas experimented with every known printing technique, continually exploring their possibilities, and here he has combined etching, aquatint, drypoint and "electric crayon" on a single plate.

absorbed the oil, but also offered the possibility of being easily cut or added to, a feature which developed his approach to the effects of design and perspective on the composition.

He was also interested in printing techniques, and experimented with every known one, from etching, drypoint, aquatint, lithography and monotype (see page 34) to "electric crayon." The latter was the carbon filament from an electric light bulb, used first at a friend's house when bad weather prevented him from leaving. He often applied color washes or pastel on top of a print, and reworked his frequently excellent first impressions. Henri Rivière maintained that, "If Degas has just been satisfied to draw on his plates quite simply, he would have left behind him the finest engravings of the nineteenth century."

Degas' eyesight had always been poor, and this may have prompted the use of pastel, as well as the choice to begin modeling in clay. From 1870 Degas had made sculptures in wax or clay, having begun by modeling horses to help him with his racecourse pictures. The figures of ballerinas evolved in a similar way, as models to aid his paintings, but later they became as important as the paintings themselves. Modeling was an invaluable tactile discipline to an artist like Degas, whose constant repetition of the same theme gave him such familiarity with his model at every angle that he was able to reproduce the subject from memory. Using clay allowed him to feel his way around the forms which his eyes had scrutinized so thoroughly. In sculpture, too, he experimented with mixed media: for instance, his wax statuette of a fourteen-year old ballerina has a blue hair ribbon and muslin tutu — he had searched also for false hair and satin ballet shoes. Mixed-media sculpture is a commonplace today, but this "clothed" bronze shocked the public in a way that his paintings had not.

Last years
Much of Degas' late work with its bold, sweeping forms and overlay of rich color springs from his failing eyesight. No longer able to create fine line drawings, his later work is a vehement slashing of color onto the roughly executed forms which years of experience, examination and sketching had etched on his mind. Blind in one eye, with the sight in the other dim, Degas was quite unmoved by the pre-war sharp rise in the sale price of his pictures, saying he felt "like a horse which has won the Grand Prix and been given another bag of oats."

DEGAS' PAINTING METHODS

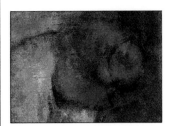

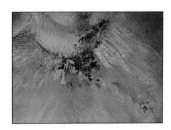

This detail from Two Laundresses *shows Degas' use of loosely handled, thinned oil paint.*

In general, Degas disliked thick paint, but he used areas of impasto to good effect, as can be seen in this detail from The Ballet Rehearsal.

The medium of pastel over monotype, seen in this detail from Dancer Curtseying, *allowed Degas to create stunning effects of color.*

Degas, unlike the Impressionists, did not favor working directly from life or painting out of doors. His concerns were with drawing, form and composition, not with the rapid recording of transient effects of light, and his chosen subject was people, not landscape. He made endless studies for his paintings, filling whole notebooks with drawings of hands, or a particular architectural feature for a background, and for his racecourse scenes he studied horses in close quarters at the Haras-du-Pin stud as well as making small clay or wax models to help him understand the animals' anatomy and the effects of motion. He believed in committing a subject to memory through repeated drawing, and when he felt he had arrived at a full understanding of it he would synthesize his many studies into a thought-out composition.

He experimented endlessly with media, often using oil paints in an unconventional way, much thinned with turpentine and applied to paper or cardboard rather than canvas. He was also greatly interested in all the printing methods — etching, lithography, drypoint and aquatint — and he virtually invented the technique of monotype (see page 34), which has been popular with artists ever since. He was at his most innovative with pastels, which he frequently used in combination with monotype, softening them over steam or mixing them with fixative to form a paint-like paste which he could then work into with a stiff brush or his fingers.

On the Beach, *1876. This work, an outdoor subject but done in the studio, was painted on paper in a medium called* peinture à l'essence. *This is oil paint drained of oil by drying and then mixed with refined turpentine, giving a matte, gouache-like consistency. It was especially suitable for preparatory studies, because it dried more quickly than ordinary oil paint, but here Degas has used it for a finished picture, with the paper mounted on canvas. He was always concerned with finding the best medium for a particular painting, and the matte paint is particularly well-suited to the flat, print-like effect, with no shadows and the minimum of modeling.*

EDGAR DEGAS
Little Dancer
c 1878-80
Tate Gallery, London

Degas began to make wax or
clay sculptures in the mid-
1870s. Their initial purpose
was to help him to understand
and paint the figure in motion,
but by the 1880s modeling had
begun to interest him as an art
form in itself. This figure of a
fourteen-year-old dancer, first
exhibited in lifelike wax and
clothed in a real muslin tutu,
shocked a public accustomed
to sculptures in stone or
bronze.

Opposite page
EDGAR DEGAS
Autumn Landscape
1890-3
Museum of Fine Arts, Boston

Landscape did not often form
part of Degas' subject matter,
but he did execute two series,
one in the middle of his life
and another toward the end.
This almost abstract work,
showing the Burgundy
countryside, is one of the later
series, which he observed
from a moving train and then
worked up in the studio, using
one of his favorite techniques
of pastel over monotype.

In 1912 his house was demolished as part of a redevelopment project, and he was obliged to move. "But since I move I no longer work," he told Daniel Halévy. "It's odd, I haven't put anything in order. Everything is there, leaning against the walls. I don't care." As his sight faded his isolation increased. "I think only of death," he confessed. A familiar, now white-bearded figure, Degas was often seen, always alone, feeling his way through the streets of Paris. Blind, solitary, but always dignified, his old age has been compared to that of the poet Homer. He died at the age of eighty-three on September 27, 1917, and his funeral, which took place toward the end of the war, was attended by those family friends who had pierced through his mask of brusqueness to the deep tenderness beneath.

Artistic aims

Degas' artistic aims were complex; he wished, he said, to produce beauty and mystery. It is not the sort of description immediately associated with the racecourse and the rehearsal room, exhausted washerwomen, deferential milliners, café-concerts, and women at their ablutions. Furthermore, this reinvention of beauty in a modern idiom is an idea that seems to fit a radical artist, not one who, born into the *haute bourgeoisie*, remained always a conservative. Degas was, in fact, a man who viewed with regret the changing society, and mourned the old values which were becoming outmoded in the new "embourgeoisement" of the capitalist class. With his intellectual astuteness, he fully realized the futility of slavishly copying the Old Masters, and he saw Symbolist art as a form of escapism, commenting derisorily that the Symbolist painter Gustave Moreau "showed us that the gods wore watch chains." It is part of the Degas paradox that the artist reared by the staunchest conservative class, from which he showed no wish to escape, should be the modern artist *par excellence*. Edmond de Goncourt observed that, "among all the artists I have met so far, he is the one who has best been able to catch the spirit of modern life."

CHRONOLOGY OF DEGAS' LIFE

1834   July 19: born in Paris, son of Auguste de Gas, a banker.

1845   Attends Lycée Louis-le-Grand.

1847   Mother dies. Father takes him to museums and fosters his gift for drawing.

1853   Studies law for a short time, then enrolls in studio of Louis Lamothe, an ex-pupil of Ingres.

1855-6   Enrolls at Ecole des Beaux Arts, Paris. Meets Fantin-Latour.

1856   Travels to Italy, staying at Rome, Naples and Florence.

1858   Visits Italy again and stays with his uncle in Florence, where he makes first studies for portrait group, *The Bellelli Family*.

1860-5   Produces several history paintings, including *Spartan Boys and Girls Exercising*.

1868   Paints *In the Orchestra Pit*.

1870   Franco-Prussian War. Called up and serves in an artillery unit in a fortress near Paris.

1872   Begins to paint the ballet, visiting rehearsal rooms of dancers.

1874   Takes part in organizing the first Impressionist Exhibition, and shows ten paintings.

1875-7   Paints *Dancer Curtseying* and *Café-concert at the Ambassadeurs*.

In the Orchestra Pit

Dancer Curtseying

The Tub

Carriage at the Races

1876   Paints *Absinthe*.

1877-90   Visits Spain. Works on etchings with Mary Cassatt and Pissarro. Paints racecourse scenes and *Miss Lala at the Circus* (1879).

1881   Shows wax statuette of dancer at sixth Impressionist Exhibition. Produces sculptures, lithographs, monotypes and pastels.

1882   Produces paintings and pastels of milliners and laundresses.

1885   Visits Le Havre and Dieppe and meets Gauguin. Eyesight worsens. Experiments with different media and concentrates on painting dancers and women at their toilet.

1886   Eighth and last Impressionist Exhibition. Shows pictures of women washing.

1893   Shows series of pastel landscapes. Eyesight continues to deteriorate, and works only with great difficulty.

1898-1912   Lives in seclusion, almost blind. House in the rue Victor Massé is demolished in 1912 and he is forced to move. His paintings are now fetching very high prices.

1917   September 27: dies at the age of eighty-three.

THE PAINTINGS

THE BELLELLI FAMILY

1858-62
79½×99½in/202×252.75cm
Oil on canvas
Musée d'Orsay, Paris

Although Degas was to paint a number of fine portraits, which in no way contradict his father's prophecy that portraiture was to become the finest jewel in his son's crown, there is no record of him ever having accepted a portrait commission; it was Degas himself who selected his sitters, and not they him. A highly accomplished painting, this work shows not only the fruits of his Italian years and the influence of sixteenth-century Florentine Mannerist art, but also his thorough grounding in the works of the Dutch masters, whom he greatly admired. The dignified pose of the baroness, the rich coloring of the interior, and the distinctive contrast of the white and black of the girl's clothing reveal a debt to the Netherlands, a debt Degas was later to acknowledge: "When we were beginning, Fantin, Whistler and myself, we were on the same path, the road from Holland." (Fantin is Fantin-Latour, the French genre and flower painter, whom Degas had met in the Café Guerbois circle.)

The legacy of his artistic mentor Ingres is also evident in the accomplished draftsmanship of the work, and there are similarities to Ingres' portrait of the Gatteaux family. However, it differs radically from that of Ingres' in that in Ingres' painting the sitters are shown to be aware of the artist, while here only the standing figure, the daughter Giovanna, can be said to acknowledge the artist. There is a sense in which we are made to feel that we are looking at the family in private, through a half-open door — an early example of Degas' predilection for viewing through a medium such as opera glasses or a camera.

Degas began to paint this picture in 1859 in the Paris studio his family had found for him in the rue Madame. Here he spread out, and assembled into a composition, the individual studies he had made of the family during his stay with them in Florence, in 1858-59. Laura Bellelli was Degas' paternal aunt, with whom he seems to have been close, for she wrote to him in Paris, "I expect you are glad to be back with your family away from my sad face and my husband's disagreeable one." Something of the strained family relations has been captured in this work. Degas remarked on the marital tensions to his uncle Achille, who replied that "The domestic life of the family in Florence is a source of unhappiness for us. As I predicted, one of them is very much at fault and our sister a little, too."

Degas has applied his uncle Achille's words, expressing the couple's estrangement not only through the faces but in the contrasted pose of the two. The baroness stands aloof and poised, like the Van Dyck Degas had admired in Genoa, protecting her daughter Giovanna. Given that this is a family portrait, the slightly hunched pose of the baron, brusquely turned away from us, is unconventional. The stare he levels at his wife, whose impenetrable gaze does not meet his eyes, intensifies the psychological tension.

As a narrative work, this painting performs a similar role to that of the history paintings Degas was engaged in at the same time. The subtext in this group portrait is the cycle of life: the baroness is in mourning for her father, René-Hilaire de Gas, Degas' grandfather (whom he drew in Naples in 1857). His portrait, by Degas, adorns the wall, and the proximity of the baroness to the portrait connects her with it. In this Degas was following an established artistic tradition, often used by the Dutch masters, of including portraits of ancestors in family portrait groups. The effect emphasizes not only the continuity of family life but of life itself. Degas' knowledge that his aunt had just become pregnant reinforces the cycle of life concept, embodied by his aunt, with the unborn child within her and an effigy of her dead father behind her. Laura herself represents the stage of adulthood, offering her protection to Giovanna.

This is an unusually large-scale work for a family portrait. The painting is not only a depiction of people — the artist's aunt, uncle and cousins — but also a social document of upper-class family life, with all the objects surrounding the sitters reflecting the lifestyle of the wealthy bourgeoisie. Beyond this, there are strong psychological nuances: Degas has subtly suggested the tension of a strained marriage from which escape meant social ostracism. Carefully planned, constructed and executed, the work shows the influence of the Old Masters while also revealing the artist's understanding of, and attraction to, tension, which is evident not only in the glance between husband and wife, but in the arrangement of figures, the composition and the play of light.

1

1 Returning home from Italy Degas was struck by Van Dyck's portrait of the Marchesa Brignole-Sale that he saw in Genoa. His notebook reveals his impressions of the work, which he has used in the portrait of his aunt. "Straight and light like a bird, her head is full of life, grace and refinement and its small, firm nose and pinched, upturned mouth. She is indeed beautiful and of a great family."

2 In contrast to his wife the Baron is sitting hunched up, turned away from the viewer. Unlike her he is in casual clothes, and presents a contemporary and urbane exterior, whereas the Baroness in her dark mourning clothes conveys a timeless nobility. The play of light which casts him in the shadow and the spatial construction which cuts him off from the family are effective devices to suggest his isolation.

3 This small triangle of pale blue is the brightest note of color in the painting, singing out against the browns, black and green-browns.

2

3

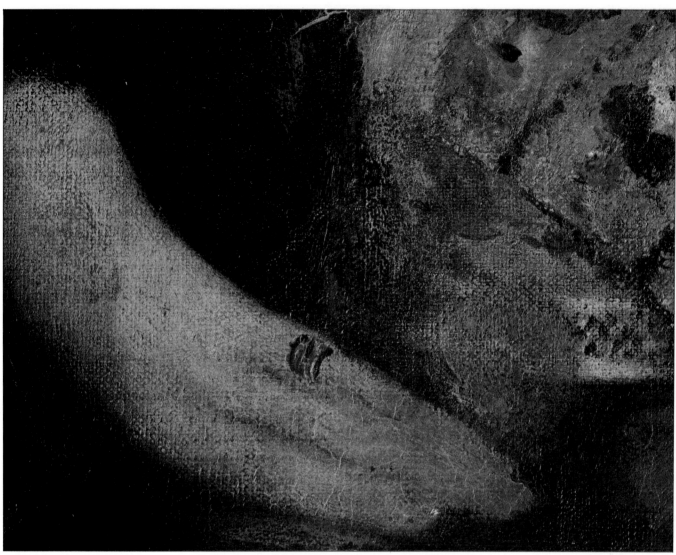

4 *Actual size detail*

4 *Actual size detail* Degas was also impressed by Van Dyck's treatment of the Marchesa's hand, which he noted as "supple and most distinguished." He made oil studies of his aunt's hands from his sketches, and George Moore has recorded him as having said, "This is my idea of genius, a man who finds hands so lovely...so difficult to render that he will shut himself in all his life, content to do nothing but indicate fingernails." The final version shows a barely modeled sweep of yellow ocher which, viewed from a distance, produces the effect of an elegant and graceful hand. Surface cracking on the dark area above reveals a light salmon pink underpaint.

5

5 One of the few extant preparatory works for his portrait, this oil study is typical of this stage of the traditional painting procedure. Having established the compositional design, Degas then made these careful studies of his aunt's hands to assist the accurate representation of them in the final work. He made minor changes to their position on the finished canvas.

IN THE ORCHESTRA PIT

1868-9

$21 \times 17\frac{3}{4}$in/53×45cm

Oil on canvas

Musée d'Orsay, Paris

This painting reflects Degas' attraction both to Japanese art and to photography. As a draftsman and admirer of Ingres he responded to the way in which the Japanese print made use of contour line, and was struck by the way in which the eastern system of perspective often silhouetted foreground objects which obscured those behind them, as happens in reality. He made the foreground obstruction something of a hallmark of his art: his café or racing scenes are often sliced by intrusive vertical devices, and in many of his pictures of the theater and ballet, columns, heads, fans or the tops of the instruments in the orchestra pit partially obscure the middle ground.

He was also attracted by the way figures in Japanese prints were often cropped, rather than being neatly contained within the picture space, and he admired the same effect in the snapshot photographs of city views which were being produced from the 1860s, which caught figures in motion moving in or out of the photo. This painting, which includes the visually blank area of the side of the orchestra box at the bottom of the painting while excluding the heads of the ballet dancers on stage, anticipates the random snapshot which has not managed to get everything in, and gives an approximation of the "frozen" view from a pair of opera glasses.

It is an artificial device used to create a reality of experience; involving the viewer by giving the sensation that we ourselves are scanning the theater, and our opera glasses have alighted on the orchestra pit. Degas maintained that, "A picture is an artificial work, something apart from nature, that demands as much cunning, astuteness and vice as the perpetration of a crime, do something artificial and add a touch of nature." The seemingly natural setting of the Paris Opera House orchestra pit has been used as a stage for a group portrait of some of the musical friends of the Degas family, not all of whom were actually in this orchestra.

The full title of the work, *Portrait of Desiré Dihau in the Orchestra Pit of the Paris Opéra*, indicates more clearly that the focus of attention is the bassoonist, a close friend of Degas' father and the main subject of the group portrait, who occupies the space usually reserved for the leader of the orchestra.

Unlike the Impressionists, with whom he dissociated himself, although exhibiting with them on numerous occasions, Degas was not interested in the effect of natural light on objects. It was artificial illumination, from gas lamps or footlights, which caught his imagination, as can be seen here, with the lower parts of the ballerinas' bodies lit to ghost-like effect by the illumination from the footlights, providing a dramatic contrast to the darkness of the orchestra pit below.

The painting, a portrait genre picture, reveals much about Degas' complex picture-making process, one which began with observation and repeated sketching until the subject was committed to memory, and was followed by the organization into a composition of his own invention. The ballerinas show the setting to be the Paris Opéra, which also housed the ballet. This is the first appearance of the dancers who were to become Degas' best-known subject.

The orchestra pit of the Paris Opéra is the setting for this portrait of Degas' friend, the bassoonist Desiré Dihau, who features prominently in an orchestra of the artist's own invention. This highly experimental composition, which dramatically decapitates the dancers and slices both sides of the orchestra, approximates to the random view from a pair of opera glasses, and suggests that this is an image the artist has actually seen rather than invented. Degas' compositions, however, were never random or unconsidered, and he was contemptuous of the notion of "instantaneous art," remarking that "what I do is the result of reflection and study of the great masters; of inspiration, spontaneity, temperament I know nothing."

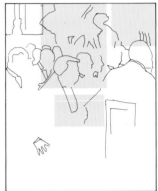

1

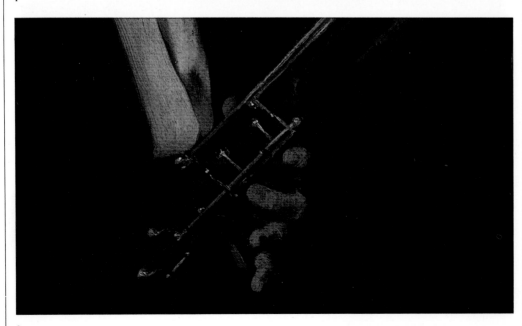

2

1 This top corner presents an impressionist cameo, intruded upon only by the bald pate of the musician. The texture of the canvas is visible beneath the dabs of thinned blue paint overlaid with touches of thicker white. Degas has evidently manipulated paint with his hands, as he did later with pastels; thumbprints are visible on the dancer's left arm.

2 This detail demonstrates Degas' fine draftsmanship as well as his virtuosity in handling paint. Dots and lines of thick white pigment have been applied over a dark area to create the effect of the instrument's metal keys and pipes. The contrast of gleaming metal on dark fabric and the contrast of white against black were effects Degas admired in the Old Masters.

3 *Actual size detail* Degas' notebooks record his interest in the effects of stage lighting. In the study of this painting he observed that near the footlight only the skirt of the dancer is lit, creating a "piquant effect." Here the ballerinas, lit to luminous intensity, provide a dramatic contrast to the prosaic figures below. In technical terms too, the divide is stressed, by the looser and more impressionistic treatment of the dancers, where shades of premixed, thinned pink pigment have been overlaid with thicker touches of white and green. The faces of the musicians are more lightly painted and fully modeled.

3 *Actual size detail*

THE BALLET REHEARSAL

c1874-6
23¼×33in/59×83.75cm
Oil on canvas
Glasgow Art Gallery, Burrell Collection

Degas is best remembered as the painter of ballet dancers, and this subject-matter constitutes half of his total output. From his mid-thirties to the end of his working life he drew, studied, modeled and painted young ballerinas, performing, rehearsing or curtseying for curtain calls; dancers seen from the auditorium, the orchestra pit, the box or the stage wings. He painted them in the rehearsal room, turning, twisting, resting, scratching, bored, and exhausted. Excited by movement and by the transformation of the skinny Parisian *rat* into graceful stage performer, the ballet provided Degas with his ideal subject matter. "It is the movement of people and things that distracts and even consoles," he remarked.

Following a visit to Degas' studio in February 1874, Edmond de Goncourt, writer, novelist and critic, assessed the artist's work in his journal. "After many experiments...he has fallen in love with the modern, and in the modern his preference goes to washerwomen and dancers...I sang the praises of both occupations as offering the most paintable models of present-day women for a modern artist." Goncourt's reference here is to his novel *Manette Salomon.* He was especially interested in the parallels between art and literature. "Here," he noted, "we see the green room at the Opéra, with dancers coming down a little staircase, their legs fantastically silhouetted against the light from a window, a bright splash of tartan amidst all those puffed-out white clouds, with the vulgar figure of an absurd ballet master to serve as foil. And there before us, caught to the life, we have the graceful, sinuous movements and gestures of these little monkey-girls."

This work is one of a series of pictures of dancers which Degas began in Paris in 1873 after his return from visiting relatives in America. When the painting was shown at a London exhibition in April 1876 it met with approval. William Michael Rossetti, writing in *The Academy,* observed, "Degas sends several pix of ballet rehearsals, as well as a number of photos somewhat less devoted to the backstairs of Terpsichore. The pictures are surprisingly clever pieces of effect, of odd turns of arrangement, and often of character, too pertinaciously divested of grace."

Rossetti has picked up on the unusual composition of the painting. Degas has left a void at the center foreground at the exact point where the principal action or figures are usually sited. The asymmetry and cropping of foreground figures reflect the influence of Japanese prints, as does the foreground obstruction of the spiral staircase on the left. The effect created is one of immediacy, giving the effect of almost placing the viewer in the rehearsal room, slightly in front of the staircase.

The work is not only a depiction of dancers exercising; it also functions as a narrative painting. The figure of the ballet master, and even more that of the tartan-shawled mother attending to one daughter with another seated at her side, contain a wealth of descriptive material. This figure echoes one of the literary themes of the day, that of mothers accompanying their daughters to their classes less to protect their virtue than to secure a good price for it.

Degas' ballet paintings over the years show a shift in viewpoint from that of distant onlooker to that of close-up recorder. It has been observed that as he watched the lengthy and exacting exercises of the ballerinas he began both to associate the dance training with that of the visual artist's training and to understand fully the nature of the toil needed for the final performance. He described his own heart in terms of the ballet, as something artificial. "The dancers have sewn it into a bag of pink satin slightly faded, like their dancing shoes."

This is an early example of the subject Degas was to make his own. He has taken a wide view from the nearside of a rehearsal room, with the dancers segregated into groups, leaving the central foreground area as simply a bare expanse of floorboard. This compositional device both gives an air of informality, and draws us into the picture in a way that a formally posed group would not. Grouping the dancers in this way is also well suited to a painting which not only depicts movement but also makes visual allusions to the off-stage life of the ballerina. Narrative detail and the evocation of atmosphere are as important in this work as abstract formal qualities.

1

2

1 The semi-transparent effect of tulle over the plaid shawl has been achieved by the use of light touches of thinned whitish pigment overlaid with greenish tones which reflect the color of the walls. The figures of the dancing master and the woman dressing the dancer caught the imagination of Edmond de Goncourt, who saw them as an intentionally comic inclusion. The red tones with which both are accentuated are balanced on the left side of the picture by the sashes of two dancers.

2 Touches of white and pink paint have been used here to capture the effect of light on the slipper and the contour of the legs. The sheen of the wooden floorboards that reflects the color of the walls may have been achieved by the scraping of applied layers of wet green pigment from a burnt orange background.

3 *Actual size detail* Lit from the left, this figure is an exercise in the gradations of light to shadow. She is caught in one of the balletic movements whose range became familiar to Degas. Edmond de Goncourt described with delight how Degas would mime the expression and movements of the dancer at her arabesques, relating "how very funny it was to see him, up on point, his arm rounded, mixing the aesthetic of the dance master with the aesthetic of the painter."

3 *Actual size detail*

DANCER CURTSEYING

c 1875

22¾ × 16½ in/58 × 42 cm

Pastel on monotype on paper

Musée d'Orsay, Paris

When asked by Mrs Havemeyer, the American collector, who bought this work in 1875, why he had concentrated on the ballet to such an extent, Degas replied, "Because I find there, Madame, the combined movement of the Greeks."

As well as full-length performances, short ballets were put on between the acts of operas. It was the moment when the talking stopped. Degas, like every Parisian gentleman of a certain rank, was a thrice-weekly visitor to the Paris Opéra. Like the majority of the audience, it was the dancers in particular he had come to see, not only on stage but behind the scenes: "From green room to wings, from the footlights to the practice-room, runs this seer, pencil in hand, hiding under his evening cloak the sketchbook where he hurriedly records some movement he has glimpsed. Then, when the lamps have been put out, he returns to his studio and there, in the sternest withdrawal, transcribes on canvas or paper the spoils gathered by his ardent eyes."

The subtle effects of tone, the contrast between the lambent delicacy of the young ballerina and the indistinct background, make this one of the artist's best-loved works. Technically it is reliant for its effect on the same technique used in the *Café Concert at the Ambassadeurs* (see page 35) and *At the Terrace of a Café* (see page 43), namely pastel over monotype. Monotype was a process which Degas had developed from standard printing techniques. The print was used rather like an underdrawing, with the pastel color applied on top, a technique which he found ideal for reproducing effects such as the ballerina's gauzy tutu, lit from the footlights and semi-transparent to reveal the lower thigh of the dancer; the sheen on her stockinged leg and the satin of her ballet slipper. The paper onto which the print has been laid is itself highly successful in approximating the patina of the stage floor.

Degas' technical achievements did not go unnoticed by the British audience when his ballet scenes were exhibited in England. The *Manchester Guardian*, in May 1876, singled out Degas' merits as a technician. "M. Degas possesses an almost perfect mastery over the secrets of tone, and he delights to exhibit the subtle changes which colour undergoes as it passes under varying conditions of light and shade. He can measure with almost absolute precision and delicacy of touch the strength of a bright sash or ribbon on the costume of the dancers as the colour flashes in the foreground or recedes into the furthest recesses of the long interior."

The composition of this work is a daring one. Now freed from the landscape format of his early history paintings, in which the action was placed squarely in the middle foreground, Degas experimented with composition, from the late 1860s preferring to use the close-up form to create a startling and immediate effect. Here we are struck by the angle from which this work is taken. If one looks at the lower triangle of the painting which contains the ballerina, she appears to be curtseying to the audience to the left of the auditorium. However, the audience seated on the left would be unlikely to see the stage wings, which would only be visible from a high point in the wings opposite or possibly from a box to the right. Clearly Degas was manipulating naturalistic detail in the interests of picture making, as he frequently did. "All art is artifice," he said, "and needs to be perpetrated with the cunning of a crime."

Degas invented what came to be called the monotype (a name he disliked) around 1874. It originated from experiments with moving printer's ink around an etching plate, either removing ink to create an image out of the blackness or drawing an image directly onto the plate and then printing. Etching itself was enjoying a revival in the 1860s, as artists were becoming dissatisfied with the dry, mechanical results of the professional printer. The works which were the result of Degas' experiments are truly innovatory, giving the lie to Renoir's remark that if Degas had been content to leave his plates alone he would have left some of the best prints of the nineteenth century. Although the name monotype suggests that only one p int was taken, Degas often took two. This second impression, the one used in this work, was paler, and provided almost a "tonal map" onto which color was added. Nearly a third of Degas' pastels show a plate mark signifying a monotype beneath.

1

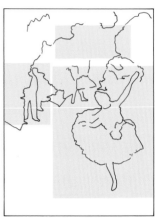

2

1 The marks of either a thumb or a stiff brush used to wipe away the printer's ink on the printing plate can be seen clearly here, overlaid with bold pastel scribbles of greens and blues. The contrast of technique seen between the loose handling of the background and the exquisite finish of the dancer prefigures the artist's later experimentation with the medium.

2 The brush or finger marks on the monotype and the ridged texture of the paper can both be seen here. The pastel application has been applied in different ways, quite lightly and patchily in the area on the left, and much more densely on the dark figure of the man. He half conceals the dancer, whose shape materializes from a few light and delicate pastel touches.

3 *Actual size detail* Degas has used brilliant white pastel on the ballet slipper, the contour of the thigh, the top of the tutu, and the throat, shoulder and hand to capture the brilliance of the footlights which highlight the dancer from below. Flowers at the waist have been realized with light touches of a pastel stick. The slightly ridged texture of the paper is clearly visible beneath a wash of background color.

3 *Actual size detail*

CAFE-CONCERT AT THE AMBASSADEURS

c1875-7
$14\frac{1}{2} \times 10\frac{1}{2}$in/$37 \times 27$cm
Pastel over monotype
Musée des Beaux-Arts, Lyon

This work is a less grand version of the scenes of the stage performance at the Paris Opéra. It is seen from immediately behind the orchestra pit. The smaller orchestra allows the inclusion of a larger section of the audience, whose gaily colored clothes and slightly caricatured treatment are reminiscent both of Daumier's cartoons of a little earlier and of the work of Toulouse-Lautrec, who was to make les Ambassadeurs his favorite haunt in the '90s.

Café life was very much part of nineteenth-century culture, and the names of many cafés have become associated with the groups of artists who met there. In 1875 Degas had moved to Montmartre, where many of the cafés put on theatrical or musical performances known as café-concerts. These shows were largely intended for the poorer, working-class section of society, and formed the proletarian counterpart to the ballet and opera attended by higher-ranking Parisians.

This work demonstrates the romantic attitude towards the working class that was not only part of the paradox of Degas' character, but also in the aristocratic tradition; a snobbish disdain toward the lower middle-class went hand in hand with an idealistic view of the workers. "I like to see the families of the working men in the Marais. You go into these wretched-looking houses with great wide doors, and you find bright rooms, meticulously clean. You can see them through the open doors from the hall. Everybody is lively; everybody is working. And these people have none of the servility of a merchant in his shop. Their society is delightful." Degas was realist enough, however, to recognize the arduous nature of their daily lives.

Degas was always attracted to the effect of artificial illumination, particularly floodlights, which produced a dramatic and violent glare from beneath, lighting those parts of the body usually shadowed — the throat, lower arm, upper lip, and knuckles and fingers of the bent hand. To give full expression to these effects, he has used one of his favorite and most interesting techniques, pastel over monotype. He was one of the great innovators in artistic media, experimenting with every known printing method. Monotype freed him from the draftsman's preoccupation with line which could have prevented him from becoming a great painter rather than a great draftsman.

The monotype process is simple and can be achieved in two ways, the subtractive or additive method. In the former, a surface such as metal or glass is coated with a greasy ink. Using a cloth or blunt instrument, the artist simply wipes or "draws away" the ink on those places which are to become light in the finished image — perfect for the creation of night-time scenes. In the second method the image is drawn directly onto the plate. In both cases it is then printed onto damp paper. The name monotype derives from the fact that only one print can normally be taken from the plate, but Degas used high-quality paper and an engraver's press rather than a hand press to create a stronger image, and this enabled him to make more than one copy, though he never took more than three. He also liked to work on a celluloid plate so that he could observe the image as it would finally appear, from the obverse side of the sheet.

Often, as in this work, he would then color the monotype with pastel. In both the printing stage and the pastel stage he avoided the use of line only by drawing with a rag or his thumb — he often used thumb-prints to achieve background texture. In the case of pastels, the very fact that they created color as well as line liberated him from the old tradition of linear modeling. The importance of color over line and form was a theme which came to dominate art in the second part of the nineteenth century.

This pastel is one of Degas' most immediately attractive works, and one in which bright color plays a dominant role. Although he dissociated himself from the Impressionists' major aims, he was undoubtedly impressed by their effective use of pure color, and the subject matter, a recreation of a scene of gaiety and pleasure, is also in the Impressionist idiom. The café concert theme was taken up in the last decade of the century by Toulouse-Lautrec, who idolized Degas. Like a great many of Degas' pastels, this one is worked over a monotype, an especially successful medium for the creation of the night-time effects which particularly interested him. "Work a great deal at evening effects, lamplight, candlelight, etc," he remarked in one of his notebooks.

1

2

1 The effect of spotlit illumination is powerfully created on the lower part of the turquoise dress. Degas has reproduced the bleached effect of strong light on fabric by means of touches of light blue and white over an area where the lines made in the monotype process are visible.

2 The lower third of the painting is in shadow, with the bottom left corner thrown into deeper shadow by dint of the illumination above, and pastel has been used over a fairly dark tonal area. There is an element of caricature in the treatment of the audience, with foreground figures quite crudely realized in contrast to the delicate handling of the figures on stage.

3 *Actual size detail* The texture and bright color of the singer's dress have been created by the classical pastel technique, the stick being applied both with bold scribbles to suggest folds or blended with finger or rag to give a smooth, tauter appearance, notably over the stomach. The effect of spotlights has been created initially on the monotype, by removing ink in the areas which were to be lightest, and then strengthened by adding highlights in pastel to the performer's lower face, arm and hand. The area around the singer's left hand clearly shows an arc of several lines which look like a thumbprint, while the white dashes which suggest illuminated leaves show similar signs of the artist's hand.

3 *Actual size detail*

ABSINTHE

c1876

$36\frac{1}{4} \times 26\frac{3}{4}/92 \times 68$cm

Oil on canvas

Musee d'Orsay, Paris

Like *In the Orchestra Pit* (see page 23) this painting, ostensibly a genre work, is in fact a portrait. The subject is Degas' friend Marcellin Desboutin at the Café de la Nouvelle-Athènes, one of his favorite spots, to which he is supposed to have introduced Degas, Manet and their circle. The focal point, however, is the seated woman at his side, the actress Ellen Andrée, who posed often for Degas and Renoir, portrayed here as a *demi-mondaine* seated before a glass of absinthe.

The sadness of this woman's situation, typical of many in both Paris and London who came into cafés either to pick up a customer or to while away the hours of loneliness with a drink, made some impact on the British public when the painting was exhibited in London in 1893. "It is not a painting at all," remarked W.B. Richmond. "It is a novelette — a treatise against drink." Clearly it is not intentionally the latter — Degas was a detached observer, not a propagandist, but the work does have literary qualities, and the woman constitutes a character study of considerable psychological depth. The downward tilt of her hat, eyes, shoulders and arms tells a story of hopelessness, and the ambiguity of her social status is reflected in her very positioning — pushed off one table and half-way between that and the next. Her isolation is intensified by the way the man at her side is turned away from her, with his forearm, a palpable barrier toward communication, occupying much of the shared table and leaving no room for her carafe of water, which is placed on the adjacent table. The tawdry gaiety of her hat and shoes adds a further note of pathos.

In terms of composition, Degas has attempted an extremely daring experiment, one that was noted and appreciated by the French critic Edmond Duranty when this work was exhibited at the second Impressionist Exhibition. "If one now considers the person, whether in a room or in the street, he is not always to be found situated on a straight line at an equal distance from two parallel objects; he is more confined on one side than on the other by space. In short, he is never in the center of the canvas, in the center of the setting. He is not always seen as a whole: sometimes he appears cut off at mid-leg, half-length, or longitudinally. At other times, the eye takes him in from close-up, at full height, and throws all the rest of a crowd in the street or groups gathered in a public place back into the small scale of the distance."

Degas has again drawn our attention to reality, to the way in which people do not sit conveniently between objects. The lower left quarter of the painting is occupied by the barren expanse of table, which not only provides an area of visual bleakness in keeping with the forlorn expression and pose of the woman, but also reflects real life and the effect of the random snapshot. Yet the composition works perfectly; the eye is led in to the figure of the woman, and the newspaper bridging the two tables not only pulls the composition together but also strengthens the naturalistic effect. Degas has placed his signature beneath the ashtray and the newspaper, almost as though claiming ownership of a patent to such a daring device. In fact it has its origins in the Japanese system of perspective, which did not rely on the Western system of distancing space into a vanishing point, but made use of foreground objects, treating the picture surface to an upward zigzag movement to suggest recession.

Probably Degas's single best-known work, this aroused strong feelings when it was shown in London. The composition is one of the artist's most daring experiments, in part derived from his observations of the Eastern system of perspective seen in Japanese prints. Degas' often-used motif of a pair of contrasting figures appears again here, but asymmetrically arranged and dramatically sliced at the right. The stasis of the two figures is emphasized by the zigzag movement of the diagonal lines formed by the outer edges of tables and newspaper, an almost abstract arrangement. The scene itself, redolent of despair and hopelessness, provides a negative counterpoint to the gaiety of café life depicted in *Café-concert at the Ambassadeurs* (see page 35).

1

2

1 To create the effect of the absinthe (a cheap but highly potent aniseed drink),light cadmium yellow has been used without modeling over dark contour lines. The stem and base of the glass are no more than a few touches of white pigment applied wet into wet over gray.

2 In this largely monochromatic portrait of Degas's friend Marcel Desboutin the face stares out, away from both his neighbor and the viewer, to a space beyond the confines of the painting. Cast in slight shadow, and more crudely modeled than that of the woman, the expression is also less psychologically probing.

3 Flush to the picture plane, the form of the ashtray is sketched out with a few bold strokes of brown and black. The newspaper bears Degas' signature almost as though it were a printed heading, a device which paradoxically draws attention by its very naturalism to the careful planning of the composition.

4 In contrast to the delicate treatment of the ballerinas' slippered feet in his paintings of dancers, this shoe is heavy and clumsy, offset by the large white bows. It is a study in monochrome, with black used for the contour lines, and touches of white applied wet into wet over gray.

5 *Actual size detail* The model for the woman was the actress Ellen André, who also posed for Renoir's more carefree and lighthearted depictions.

3

4

5 *Actual size detail*

AT THE TERRACE OF THE CAFE

c 1877
16×23¼in/41×59cm
Pastel over monotype
Louvre, Paris

Degas encapsulated the gaiety and pathos of lower-class café life; a contemporary recorder observed that "M. Degas is observant, he never seeks to exaggerate, his effects are always obtained by nature itself, with no element of caricature. It is this that makes him the most graceful historian of the scenes he shows us. Here we have some women outside the door of a café, at night: one of them is tapping her teeth with her fingernail and saying 'pas seulement ça,' a poem in itself. Another is spreading out her large gloved hand on the table. In the background is the boulevard, its bustle slowly dying away. This is a very striking historical record."

Degas himself said, "In a single brushstroke we can say more than a writer in a whole volume." His ability to distil the essence of life around him impressed contemporary authors, particularly Emile Zola, who much admired this work of the demimonde, and in 1879 put out in serial form his novel *Nana*, a story about a former laundress turned musical performer-cum-actress and prostitute. However, although Degas' paintings have been described in literary terms, he was far from a literary painter, and was irritated by dinner-party conversations on art. "Let us hope that we shall soon have finished with art, with aesthetics. They make me sick...what interests me is work..." "Degas liked talking about painting," said Paul Valéry, "but could hardly bear anyone else doing so." He derided critics, "thinkers" and the "literary gentry" who wrote about art, maintaining that form and color, not words, were the medium best suited to conveying the artist's intentions.

In this work, as in several others, he has used pastel over monotype (see page 34), a technique well suited to creating night-time effects, particularly artifically lit ones. "Daylight is too easy," he remarked, "What I want is difficult — the atmosphere of lamps or moonlight." He began here by painting a general outline of the main forms onto a flat surface which he then printed onto paper, adding color and detail with the pastels. The subdued color suggests not only the dimness of evening lighting, but also the somber world of his subject. Painted in the studio from memory, the work is a keenly observed social portrait as well as an attempt at finding fresh ways of looking at contemporary life. Like the female figure in *Absinthe* (see page 39), the expression of the central blue-clad figure speaks volumes.

The vertical slicing of the picture by the pillars of the café provides a dramatic fragmentation of the picture surface, an appropriately startling compositional device for the "shocking" subject-matter of casually observed street-walkers conversing together, and the way figures and chairs at the edges of the picture have been cropped effectively places the viewer in the picture with the women. The severity of the pillars has been offset by the undulating rhythm formed by the tops of the women's hats, their shoulders and chair backs, as well as by the muted but glowing color and texture of the clothing.

The monotype print beneath the pastel is more in evidence here than in *Café Concert at the Ambassadeurs* (see page 35), indeed, apart from white highlights and a touch of blue and light brown, the upper half at least is almost monochromatic — essentially a print that has not been transformed by color. Similarly, the lower half of the painting, containing the women, registers as a low-key study in blue and brown with cream lights in the hats and flesh tones of the faces, pure color being reserved for the flowers on the hat to the far right. In collecting material for this work Degas was apparently even more meticulous than in the case of *Absinthe* (see page 39), recording in his notebooks the exact shapes of chairs, hats and figures, and making careful notes of the subtle variations of lighting effects he had observed on the terrace. The narrative quality of the work has evoked a number of literary parallels, among them a suggestion that the work is an illustration from Ludovic Halévy's novel *La Famille Cardinal*, although no passage corresponds very closely.

1

2

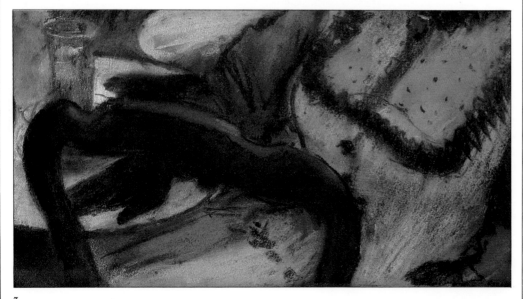

3

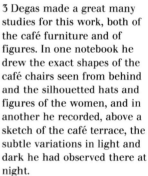

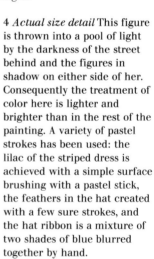

1 The two faces on the left are barely modeled, but that on the extreme left is a good portrait achieved with just a few sure strokes.

2 In contrast to the subdued tone of the picture the artificial flowers on the hat are made up from three primary colors, plus green and lilac, applied with a degree of detail largely absent in the rest of the work. It is the only area of pure color, almost a polychromatic "joke" slapped onto the end of the painting like a punchline.

3 Degas made a great many studies for this work, both of the café furniture and of figures. In one notebook he drew the exact shapes of the café chairs seen from behind and the silhouetted hats and figures of the women, and in another he recorded, above a sketch of the café terrace, the subtle variations in light and dark he had observed there at night.

4 *Actual size detail* This figure is thrown into a pool of light by the darkness of the street behind and the figures in shadow on either side of her. Consequently the treatment of color here is lighter and brighter than in the rest of the painting. A variety of pastel strokes has been used: the lilac of the striped dress is achieved with a simple surface brushing with a pastel stick, the feathers in the hat created with a few sure strokes, and the hat ribbon is a mixture of two shades of blue blurred together by hand.

4 *Actual size detail*

CARRIAGE AT THE RACES

1877-80

26×32¼in/66×82cm

Oil on canvas

Musée d'Orsay, Paris

Around 1860-63 Degas had begun to develop new interests and friendships such as those with Duranty and Manet, and the circle of artists at the Café Guerbois. Themes of realism were much discussed in literary and artistic circles, and this climate had an important effect on Degas, leading him toward the kind of contemporary subject-matter advocated by the writer and poet Charles Baudelaire.

Degas was not especially interested in racing as such — he accompanied Manet to the races as another well-to-do young man amusing himself — but he found the horse a wonderful mechanism of moving muscle. He had included horses in his earliest history paintings such as *The Misfortunes of the City of Orléans*, and had studied them in works of the Old Masters. A stay at Menil-Hubert, the chateau of his schoolfriend Paul Valpinçon, where the surrounding countryside resembled that in English sporting prints, and a visit to the nearby stud of Haras-du-Pin, the most celebrated breeding establishment of the day, brought him into close quarters with the animal, which he began to study in detail, making little models in wax and clay to help him understand the effects of motion.

The poet Paul Valéry noted that Degas was "one of the first to study the true forms of noble animal in movement by means of the instantaneous photographs of Major Muybridge." The publication in *The Globe* of Eadweard Muybridge's photographs of horses in motion (see opposite) in 1881 confirmed Degas' own photographic observations that horses did not fly through the air when galloping as English sporting prints had shown them to do. Degas was one of the first artists to show an interest in photography.

Soon after Degas' death in 1917, Jacques-Emile Blanche commented on his innovative system of composition based on the snapshot. "The instantaneous photograph with its unexpected cutting-off, its shocking differences in scale, has become so familiar to us that the easel paintings of that period no longer astonish us...no one before Degas ever thought of doing them, no one since has put such 'gravity'...into the kind of composition which utilizes to advantage the accidents of the camera."

Degas copied his horses from a variety of sources: not only from the stud and racecourse themselves, but from the Parthenon frieze, the paintings of Uccello and Gozzoli, the great Dutch masters, the French Romantic artists, English sporting prints, his own sculptures and, after 1881, from Muybridge's photos published in *Animal Locomotion*. The seemingly arbitrary agreement of mounted horses milling around before or after the race is in fact a "stealthy act of premeditated instantaneity." As Degas said, "Nothing should seem like an accident."

Jean Cocteau expanded on Degas' debt to the photograh in *Le Secret Professionnel* (1922). "Among our painters Degas was the victim of photography as the Futurists were victims of cinematography. I know photographs by Degas which he enlarged himself and on which he worked directly in pastel, marveling at the composition, the foreshortening, the distortion of the foreground forms."

There is no cutting-off in Degas' earlier pictures of racecourse scenes. The device was probably first used in his *Jockeys at Epsom* of 1862, after which it became frequent, especially in the depiction of movement, as in pictures of horses or dancers, where the cropping of figures suggests continuous movement outside and beyond the picture plane. His full mastery of the racecourse as a subject is evident between 1878-91. These scenes of the race are the nearest Degas comes to outdoor painting, until the series of pastels toward the end of his life (see page 15).

Degas' earliest works on the theme of racing show a broader perspective than this painting, and include not only the jockeys on their horses but also the spectators and racecourse. Here he has included a carriage and just a glimpse of the racegoers, and the composition is not unlike that of *The Ballet Rehearsal* in that the left foreground is totally devoid of figures at precisely the spot where a traditional painter would have placed them.

EADWEARD MUYBRIDGE
Horse in Motion

Muybridge's photographs, published in *Animal Locomotion* in 1881, showed that horses did not gallop with all four legs outstretched as they had appeared in English sporting prints and in Degas' own earlier work. Degas, who was interested in photography and owned his own camera, was quick to adjust to Muybridge's observations and incorporate them into his later depictions of horses.

1

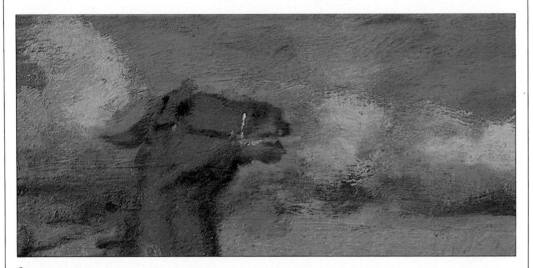

2

3

1 Degas' generalized landscape is probably of his own invention rather than a true representation. It is basically a monochrome tonal study, in gray with touches of black and white, but the slope of the hillside is suggested by broad planes of green overlaid with a thin terracotta glaze.

2 During 1859-69 Degas made copies from a wide variety of sources representing the horse, and from the stock of poses he amassed he was able to make a selection for his oils and pastels on this theme. The head of the galloping horse is not unlike one of Delacroix' wild, flared-nostrilled chargers. The billowing steam from a passing train, paralleling the course of the animal, is unique in Degas' work, and provides a neat juxtaposition of modernity and classicism.

3 The lower left corner of the painting is occupied by a cropped close-up of the carriage wheels. The monochromatic use of grays, used in a lighter shade for the man's jacket, is reminiscent of Manet, who was an important influence on Degas in the 1860s.

4 *Actual size detail* Degas was interested in the counterbalance of pairs of figures, and here the two overlapping jockeys create a rhythmic directional thrust which tightens the composition at the right of the picture. The cracks on the man's hat are the result of overpainting before the underlayer was fully dry.

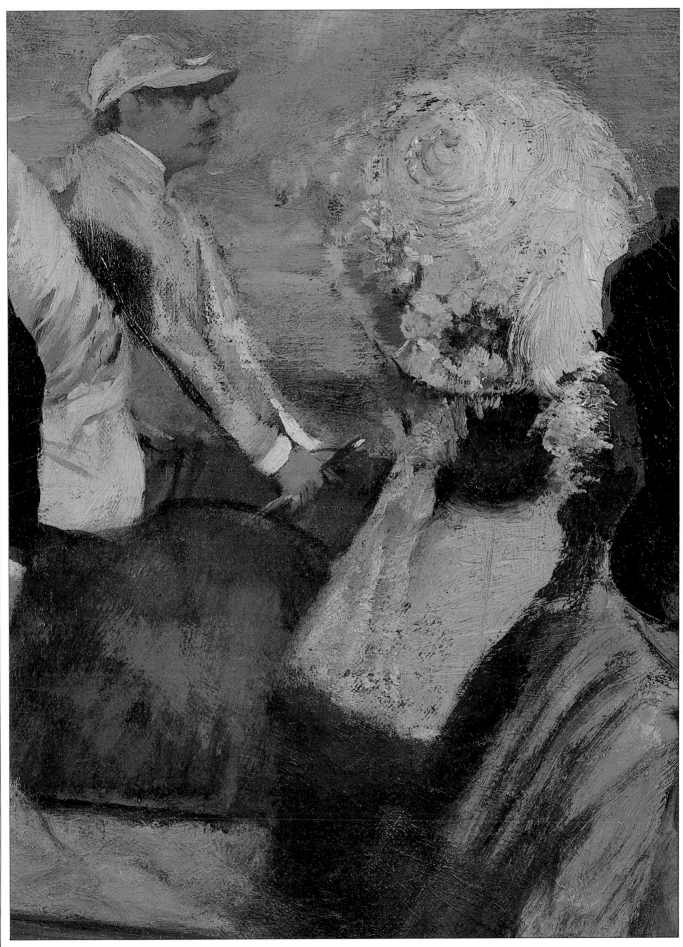

4 *Actual size detail*

MISS LALA AT THE CIRCUS

1879
46×30½in/117×77.5cm
Oil on canvas
National Gallery, London

Degas made numerous studies of Miss Lala, a mulatto circus artiste whose sensational feats were enthusiastically received when she and her troupe performed in Paris at the Cirque Fernando in January 1879. Known as "La Femme Canon," she held a cannon on a chain between her teeth while hanging by her legs from a trapeze. The cannon was subsequently fired. This and other staggering displays depended principally upon her extraordinary teeth and jaw muscles. Here Degas has chosen to depict her being hoisted to the rafters of the circus pavilion by means of a rope in her mouth. The *Westminster Review* gave a colorful description of Miss Lala's London Performance. "During the past week an additional attraction has been added in the person of a dusky lady know as La La, whose feats of strength fairly eclipse anything and everything of the kind that has gone before. She does all that her muscular rivals have done and a great deal more. She has we believe already astonished Paris, and we have little doubt that her fame in London will rapidly spread."

The choice of the circus as a subject, like that of the café concert, reflects the shift of artistic subject matter from the "elevated" — history or myth — to modern life. Degas was particularly attracted to the artificial in contemporary subject-matter, a preference he acknowledged to an Impressionist landscape painter he met at the circus. "For you, natural life is necessary; for me, artificial life."

His enthusiasm for *The Zemganno Brothers*, Edmond de Goncourt's novel which describes the skilled performance of circus acrobats, demonstrates the inter-dependence of art and literature and the way in which both frequently made use of the same subject matter. Degas, however, was less interested in recreating the atmosphere of places of popular entertainment than in using the settings as a basis for the arrangement of abstract shapes. The exclusion of the audience in favor of a close-up of the performer diminishes the frisson of danger and sense of vertigo which another artist might have stressed.

Like Manet, Degas was basically an abstract artist using the human figure onto which to project form and color. Interested more in the arrangement of shapes than in the exact reproduction of what was before his eyes, he sought to invest his painting with a "magic ingredient." This was the result, not of catching an immediate and passing effect, but of recreating, by a process of observation, sketching and synthesis, something of his own reaction to his subject. Huysmans was impressed by the way Degas had altered the inclination of the circus walls to enhance an effect, and Degas' notebooks show him to have been fascinated by the rafters of the ceiling, its architectural members and surface decoration, for which he made many sketches annotated with details of structure and color. "La Femme Canon" herself appears to have been a useful model for depicting from below, another effect that his notebooks show he was aiming at. "After painting portraits seen from above, I am now going to paint some seen from below."

More than any other artist of the last century, Degas was an artist who sought to master his craft by means of experimentation with media. This investigative approach was one that extended to his subject matter, usually the human form, which he sought to understand by means of intense observation and drawings, made from as many different viewpoints as possible. The circus, where the sphere of action is often above the spectator, offered him the perfect opportunity for depicting the model from below as well as providing a contemporary yet exotic note.

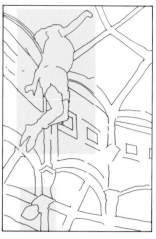

1 Degas was interested in the effect of superimposing the human form over the architectural features, providing an interesting contrast between the rounded forms of the performer herself and the linear, almost gridlike pattern made by the rafters, beams, windows and windowsills. Huysmans, writing in *L'Art Moderne* in 1880 of this work, which was exhibited at the fourth Impressionist Exhibition in 1879, was impressed by the artist's ingenuity. "In order to give the exact sensation of the eye following Miss Lola [sic], climbing to the very top of the Cirque Fernando, Degas dared to make the circus roof lean wholly to one side."

2 *Actual size detail* The artist's notebooks not only reveal his interest in the structure of the pavilion and its gilded stucco decoration but contain detailed annotations of the color harmonies of the interior. Degas made three attempts at the roof, each in a different medium, before bringing together his observations of the artiste in her lofty setting. With a few light, sure touches he has achieved the effect of green-painted acanthus leaf on the slender column.

1

2 Actual size detail

TWO LAUNDRESSES

1882

30×32¼in/76×82cm

Oil on canvas

Musée d'Orsay, Paris

Degas painted and drew laundresses — ironers and washerwomen — over a thirty-three year period from about 1869 to 1902. Like the ballerinas, they obsessed him. Visiting relatives in New Orleans in 1872 he wrote home, "Everything is beautiful in this world of people. But one Paris laundry girl, with bare arms, is worth it all for such a pronounced Parisian as I am." Clearly the Parisian laundress was for Degas a symbol of the city, if not the country as whole: "Long live fine laundering in France," he cheered in a letter to a close friend. The image of the laundress abounded in the literature and art of the time, and not surprisingly, since it was reckoned that one fifth to a third of the work force was occupied in the laundry business.

Laundresses were, moreover, subjects of sexual titillation in period literature and popular art, and Degas' remarks, unusually for him, also hint at this. They worked in small rooms, oppressively hot, and they usually stripped down to their stays or even further for the sake of comfort. Their bare arms and frequent state of undress attracted the attention of passing custom, and made them in the popular mind women of easy virtue.

Edmond de Goncourt maintained that they were, along with ballerinas, "the most paintable models of modern women," and he praised the artist's trained eye which could reproduce the very strokes of the iron. "Degas brings washerwomen before our eyes, while speaking their very language, giving us technical explanations about when to press down on the iron, when to make a circular movement with it, etc."

Degas has not chosen to glamorize the arduous life of a laundress, but nor does he make her an object of pathos, as a more politically oriented painter might have done. He has treated his subject-matter with detachment, using the figures to construct an almost abstract balance of form — one leaning over, face indistinct, arms straight, pressing with both hands; the other leaning back, yawning, arms relaxed, away from the body. As with his studies of dancers, Degas was at this time interested in the counterbalance of figures.

In pictures of washerwomen and ballet dancers he made the *jolie-laide* his hallmark. The figure on the left, yawning inelegantly and clutching the neck of a bottle of wine — frequent comforter of the hard-pressed ironer — is double-chinned, snub-nosed and wide-nostrilled, far removed from the popular saucy, sexy images.

It is a work of finely tuned balance — that between disposition of the figures themselves, and that between sentimentalizing and overstating — and all superfluous detail is eliminated, making a pictorial parallel with the dictum of the poet Stephane Mallarmé that all that was not strictly necessary should be banished from art. The use of color warms the surroundings of the figures, and lends something of the atmosphere of old paintings to this essentially modern treatment. Degas disliked thick paint, which is hardly surprising in one who was above all else a draftsman, but the puritan in him may also have suspected the sensuality of thick paint — his father had warned against Delacroix the colorist. Here we can see how he has applied background color in single strokes which barely cover the canvas, but has built up layers of pigment in the figures, producing a subtlety of color and richness of texture in the clothing that transforms these simple laundresses, an emblem of the everyday, into a modern classic.

The simplicity of this painting, as in all of Degas' work, is deceptive. "Nothing," he insisted, "should appear accidental, not even movement." Background detail is discarded, and the figures take on a monumental importance, a suggestive quality which recognizes the arduous nature of the work yet transcends it into a modern icon. Color is broken and mixed in dull harmonies; no strong lights or darks disrupt the dominant middle tone. Degas admired the effect of old frescoes, and often sought to reproduce their subtle quality by scraping off the wet paint from the canvas, leaving a residue held by the texture of the support. Scraping down when dry gives a slightly different quality, veiled and suggestive. Degas disliked the oiliness of what he called "licked paintings," and he often removed the oil from his paint and thinned it with turpentine. His paint application is unusual, thin and matte, with the bare canvas clearly visible, the treatment suggesting the steam-filled room.

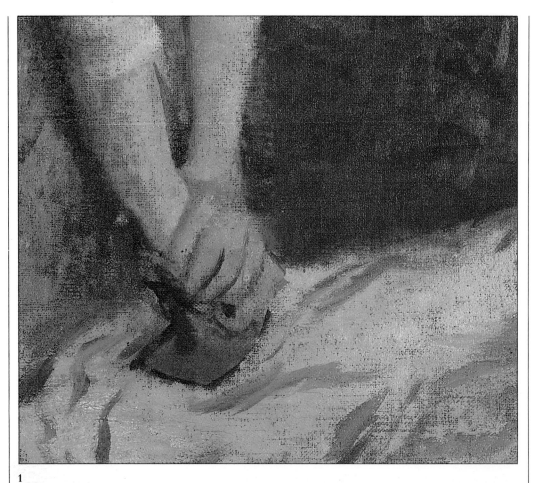

1

2

1 Degas could reproduce the movements of the ironer, like those of the dancer, from memory, having studied them exhaustively. Here he has caught the gesture of left hand pressing over right for maximum effect. A dark contour line has been used, both as the preliminary drawing and to provide an outline over the painted form. The treatment of the iron and shirt is different to that in the rest of the painting where colors are applied in a semi-transparent glaze or are broken into strange harmonies.

2 "Relief should be flat," remarked Degas, hinting at his loathing of *trompe l'oeil* effects, and in this semi-transparent still life, form has been flattened in conformity with his axiom. The shot colors of the skirts are probably the result of a layered application and scraping down of paint, and suggest a tapestry, an effect the artist chose to emulate. "I remember a certain oriental rug I had seen in the Place Clichy," he told a friend who had asked him whence he derived his color harmonies.

3 *Actual size detail* The planes of the face have been suggested by a subtle handling of light color in the same tonal range. The texture of the bare canvas is apparent, overlaid with loosely handled thinned pigment which creates an impression of steam.

3 *Actual size detail*

THE TUB

1886

$23\frac{5}{8} \times 32\frac{5}{8}$ in/61×82.5cm

Musée d'Orsay, Paris

"The nude has always been represented in poses which presupposed an audience, but these women of mine are honest, simple folk, unconcerned by any other interests than those involved in their physical condition. Here is another, she is washing her feet. It is as though you looked through a keyhole." Degas' remark to George Moore, a rare studio visitor, testifies to his proclivity for depicting scenes as though through an invisible spy-hole. It is an extension of the artist's protective mask to view unseen, as well as a revelation of his often rather harsh voyeuristic characteristics.

The observation of his studies of the female nude was prefaced by the remark, "She is the human animal attending to itself, a cat licking herself." Toward the end of his life Degas confessed that he had perhaps treated the study of women too dispassionately. The novelist and critic Huysmans wrote that Degas had "with his studies of nudes, contributed a lingering cruelty, a patient hatred."

"It seems as though, exasperated by the baseness of his surroundings, he has resolved to proceed to reprisals and fling in the face of his own century the grossest insult, by overthrowing woman, the idol which has always been so gently treated and whom he degrades by showing her naked in the bathtub, in the humiliating positions of her private toilet...Here we have a red-head, dumpy and stuffed, back bent, so that the sacrum bone sticks out from the stretched bulging buttocks; she is straining to curl her arm over her shoulder so as to squeeze a sponge, the water from which is trickling down her spine and splashing off the small of her back.

"Such, in brief, are the merciless positions assigned by this iconoclast to the being usually showered with fulsome gallantries.

"But in addition to this special accent of contempt and hatred, what one should note in these works is the unforgettable truthfulness of the types caught with a simple, basic style of drawing, with lucid, controlled passion, coldly but feverishly; what one notes is the warm, veiled color of these scenes, their rich, mysterious tone, the supreme beauty of flesh turning to blue or pink under the water, lit by closed muslin-draped windows in dark rooms where the dim light from a courtyard reveals washbasins and bathtubs, bottles and combs, the glazed boxwood backs of brushes, pink copper hot-water jugs."

Huysmans has expanded on the way Degas' drawing and subtle color transformed the ugly and everyday, an effect much helped by pastel. Although Degas had used the medium in the 1860s, it was from the '70s onward that he began to take full stock of its possibilities, experimenting with methods of fixing what is essentially colored chalk onto the picture surface. The richness of much of his pastel work was greatly admired by Renoir, who personally found the medium uncongenial, but noted that in Degas' hands it possessed "the freshness of fresco." For a draftsman it was the most successful medium for transforming line into color. The two happened simultaneously: in this work contours are clearly visible, showing that Degas was still working principally with line, but the overlay of white highlight and darker shadow tones mitigate the outline effect.

This nude is a modern-day Susannah at her bath. Degas made this connection himself while at the same time denying it. "See what differences time has brought. Two centuries ago I would have painted Susannah at her bath. Today, I paint only women at their tubs." The work is a successful reinterpretation of the Old Masters in the modern idiom. In a way Degas was a painter of modern life in spite of himself, taking to heart Baudelaire's dictum that "the man who does not accept the conditions of ordinary life sells his soul," while at the same time lamenting an age gone by. "They were dirty perhaps, but distinguished; we are clean but we are common."

Women at their toilette was one of Degas' most favored subjects at this stage of his life, and he sketched them from many viewpoints and in every aspect — getting in and out of the bath, washing and drying themselves, and having their hair brushed. In this work the angle of the close-up viewpoint is unusual: seen from above, the table and shelf has become an abstract slice of the picture, its strong, almost vertical line which traverses the height of the canvas broken by the handle of the brush and copper jug. This daring compositional device, which is found in a number of Degas' works, is a deliberate break with a classically inspired arrangement. The radical treatment of the nude, not as an idealized thing of beauty but as a working woman washing herself, presented a shock to visitors at the eighth Impressionist Exhibition. In Huysmans' eyes it was a deliberate attempt to shock the *bourgeoisie,* who, he commented, "cried out, indignant at this frankness, struck all the same by the life flowing from these pastels. In the end they exchanged some doubtful or disgusted comments and upon leaving, their parting shot was: 'It's obscene'."

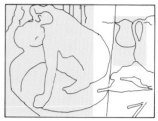

1

1 Denis Rouart noted that Degas adapted to pastel "the technique of making colors play against each other by superimposition and transparency rather than merely by the opposition of areas of color. Transparency could not, of course, be obtained in pastel as it could be with glazes in oil paint; so he arrived at an analogous effect by working in successive layers, not covering the lower layer entirely but letting it show through." Rouart also described the way in which Degas would lay in his subject in pastel, spray boiling water over it to make the dry pastel into a paste, and then work into it with brushes to varying stiffness. "He took care not to spray the water vapor all over the picture, so as to keep the original surface of the pastel where he wanted to give it variety."

2 *Actual size detail* Gone are the alluring feminine accoutrements of an Old Master "Susannah Bathing," with her ivory-handled scissors, silver-framed hand-mirror and string of pearls. Instead we have the real articles of the female toilette, not intended for public display — the false hairpiece, curling tongs, cheap wooden-handled brush, copper hot-water jug and serviceable cold water pitcher.

2 *Actual size detail*

INDEX

Photographic Credits
Boston Museum of Fine Arts 15; Bridgeman Art Library, London 8,
14; Chicago Art Institute 12; Durand-Ruel & Cie, Paris 9; Glasgow
Art Gallery 27-29; Hubert Josse, Paris 19-21, 23-25, 31-33, 39-41, 43-
45, 47-49, 55-57, 59-61; Musée des Beaux Arts, Lyon 35-37; National
Gallery, London 10, 13, 51-53; Nelson-Athins Museum of Art, Kansas
City 11; Service photographique de la Réunion des musées
nationaux, Paris 6, 7 left and right.

DATE DUE

MA ████████	